HUMANOID ROBOT

What you should know.

MAC HUDSON

TABLE OF CONTENTS

CHAPTER 1: WHAT IS A HUMANOID ROBOT

Humanoid robots are professional service robots developed to replicate human movements and interactions. Like other service robots, they deliver value by automating duties in a manner that leads to cost savings and productivity. Humanoid robots are a relatively new sort of professional service robot. While long-dreamt of, they're now beginning to become economically feasible in a broad variety of applications.

The humanoid robotics industry is set for significant expansion. It's anticipated that the market for humanoid robots will be valued at $3.9 Billion in 2023, expanding at a stunning 52.1% compound annual growth rate (CAGR) between 2017 and 20231. Of all the forms of humanoid robots, bipedal robots are predicted to expand at the quickest CAGR throughout the forecasted period. The fast rise of the humanoid robotics market is attributable mostly to the constantly developing capabilities of these robots and their usefulness in an ever-widening variety of applications.

Humanoid robots are being employed in the inspection, maintenance and emergency response at power plants to relieve human employees of hard and risky jobs. Similarly, they're poised to take over ordinary chores for astronauts in space flights. Other various uses include providing companionship for the elderly and ill, serving as a guide and engaging with clients in the function of receptionist, and maybe even becoming a host for the development of human transplant organs.

There's a vast variety of duties a humanoid robot can automate, from perilous rescues to caring care. How these robots are used is continually growing, and as the underlying technology improves, the market will follow pace.

Humanoid robot research for the actual evaluation of motor learning

Recently, multiple research groups have begun to examine "Humanoid" robots from diverse angles. One of the current works is involved with trajectory creation for walking, dancing or leaping actions. A complete-body humanoid robot was constructed to produce numerous forms of human-like movements. It is a self-contained type of humanoid robot. It can independently walk on relatively uneven ground. Humanoid robots are being researched as communication devices. Another innovative research is the Cog project at MIT and the Humanoid robot project at the Waseda Univ. Both research organizations concentrate on examining cognitive behaviour using their humanoid robots. The combination of psychology, neuroscience and robotics in such initiatives appears to be quite beneficial from both a technical and biological point of view.

One of the most exciting study fields for neuroscience and robotics research is the idea of motor learning in humans, and humanoid robots may successfully be utilized to confirm research theories. What sorts of capabilities are required for a humanoid robot in such a study area? One of the most significant qualities is that kinematics and dynamics are comparable to people, e.g., that weight, size, location of the centre of the mass, and preferably the viscoelastic properties of the joints are human-like. Equally crucial is the availability of sensory input to emulate human proprioception and that joint torques may be created to achieve human levels of performance, but also human constraints.

CHAPTER 2: ADVANTAGES AND DISADVANTAGES OF HUMANOID ROBOTS.

Humanoid Robots can be used in everyday life to do jobs that people do not want to do, they can do them more efficiently, they will become more adept over time, and they will do many tasks that humans do now cheaply and easily, it is a great challenge in robotics to build robots that do things like humans in a world made for humans, they can move and perform well-designed tasks. These are the advantages and disadvantages of the robot.

ADVANTAGES OF THE HUMANOID ROBOT

Humanoid robots will be useful to many people around the globe, We can use these robots for educational purposes as well, Robotics is being used by teachers to help instruct students on how to program, Robot teacher is also used to interact with children and teach them to do simple tasks.

Many people will benefit from these humanoid robots; they will care for the sick, collect garbage, defend homes and businesses, and provide instructions on the street. Life in society with Humanoid Robots will be tremendously different, but highly efficient, and the economy will improve.

Corporations and businesses will also be appreciative of the robots because they could use them to replace jobs, This means less money that businesses will have to fork out to their employees, They can be used as entertainers & in commercial spaces but they will not undertake major tasks, These robots can do amazing things that even people could not do, They can now sing & dance and look almost like the human when doing so.

The human body is very difficult to imitate and there is much more work to be done. They can be beneficial in assisting elderly people living in their own homes to respond to disasters. There are remarkable advancements and quick growth in the engineering and control elements of humanoid robots.

Humanoid robots can be used to assist the military. They can move, gather information (via sensors) in the real world, and interact with it. They do not yet have some features of the human body. They include structures with variable flexibility, which offer safety (to the robot and the people), and redundancy of movements.

Humanoid Robots can operate in factories and perform the same thing over & over again and without any change, Humans, on the other hand, would become weary after doing the same thing repetitively and might easily make a mistake.

Humanoid Robots can accomplish many things that humans can do and even things that people are unable to do, The sale & development of these Humanoid Robots will help expand the economy, Having these robots will make firms more efficient in their job and drive the economy with their revenue growth.

Humanoid Robots do not make the errors that are valuable to certain nations, They prefer to have the robots perform menial work rather than low-paid immigrants from other countries, The people like the robots since they do not make mistakes and there is no opportunity for them to be impolite.

Humanoid Robots can be used with children, they can be used to teach or read to children, they can greatly assist children with autism, they can assist the sick and elderly, they can be used in dirty or dangerous jobs, and they are suitable for some procedurally-based vocations, such as reception-desk administrators and automotive manufacturing line workers, they can use the tools and operate equipment and vehicles designed for the human form.

A significant advancement in science and technology has resulted in advanced humanoid mechatronic systems that are rich in complex sensorimotor capabilities. It is an emerging and challenging research field that has received significant attention in recent years and will continue to play a central role in robotics research.

DISADVANTAGES OF HUMANOID ROBOT

A humanoid robot is quite costly, depending on how sophisticated the robot is, As the humanoid robot starts becoming more and more available to society, it will be mostly the wealthy who will be able to afford them, It will replace the jobs, Although this will be beneficial to many companies, it will hurt those who have jobs in certain fields, such as nurses, pharmacists, secretaries, etc.

The sophisticated humanoid robots will be able to do a range of duties, But they cost a lot of money, For middle-class & low-income families, It is a high expense that many people can't afford, The price of humanoid robots is high enough that everyone can't own one, one of the common problems tackled in the humanoid robotics is the understanding of the human-like information processing and the underlying mechanisms of the human brain in dealing with the real world.

If you have these robots doing these everyday jobs for you, You will become too dependent on robots, If you have the robots that will take out the trash, do the dishes, cook the food, watch the children, You will become lazy, and dependent if you have such robots doing your chores for you, This is another downfall of the evolving "humanoid robot."

A lot of people will suffer from the humanoid robot, Humanoid robot will replace their employment, Middle class and low-income families would be harmed by the robots, Although most of the upper class will be able to have these humanoid robots to perform certain activities that they don't want to do, middle-class families will not be able to purchase them meaning that they are stuck doing the tedious tasks themselves.

Many occupations can be replaced by automation technologies & robots, The humanoid robots will one day replace the employment of middle-class humans, They will assume practically all conventional labour tasks in society including firefighting, restaurant service, manufacturing, agriculture, construction, & community police, If the humanoid robots take over middle-class folks employment, our economy will be badly damaged.

CHAPTER 3: FACTS ABOUT HUMANOID ROBOTS.

With breakthroughs in artificial intelligence, computers are learning to not only execute human activities but also go far beyond. However, for humans and robots to work together more smoothly, machines need to inhabit the same area and humanoids are the finest platforms to achieve this. The top 5 frightening facts concerning humanoid robots.

1. Most Human-like Robots Are Female.

From Nadine through Sophia you will discover most of the humanoids are female. Because women are viewed as warmer and more prone to feel emotions than males, the feminine gendering of AI objects helps to humanise them. Warmth and experience (but not ability) are certainly recognized as important attributes to be a whole person but are absent in robots.

2. Ideology to Destroy Humans.

In several interviews, it has been observed that human-like robots have harmful ideas and aim to either destroy or rule people. Is it conceivable for a robot to govern humans? Possibilities are unlimited, and continually expanding technology may put mankind in danger.

3. Robot Can Read Your Mind.

Scary right? New technology has been created by roboticists that can build a picture of your thoughts using an fMRI scanner. The Robot is meant to generate an image from your brain and compare it with other photos obtained from volunteers.

4. Human-Like Robots Have Nationalities and Passports.

Sophia, a realistic robot has obtained guaranteed citizenship in Saudi Arabia. This has created great debate as the public wonders and asks whether or not robots should have rights. The basic objective of artificial intelligence is for humans to have a computer that thinks quicker and more effectively.

5. Robots to Take Away Jobs.

While the robot revolution isn't eliminating everyone's jobs, automation is taking some of them, particularly in industries such as manufacturing. And it's simply making work different: A machine may not remove a position, but it may change a more middle-skill job into a low-skill one, bringing lower income with **it**

CHAPTER 4: FUTURE PROSPECT OF HUMANOID ROBOTS.

Humanoid robots will become more prevalent in the robotics sector, but do they have a place in the engineering industrial sector or are they simply a fad?

Over the next ten years, there will be more robots, as has been well-documented. The Boston Consulting Group predicts that by 2025, 25% of all labour-intensive jobs will be carried out by robots. This is a result of cost- and performance-related improvements. The adoption of robots will be driven by the United States, Canada, Japan, South Korea, and the United Kingdom. Computer and electronic items, electrical equipment and appliances, transportation equipment, and machinery are the four sectors that are leading the way. By 2025, they will represent 75% of all robotic deployments.

The service sector will be impacted by the development of robots. The service robot base is anticipated to install 264.3 million units by 2026, according to a recent analysis by Berg Insight. Globally, 29.6 million service robot installations were made in 2016. The robots in the service sector split down into the following groups:

Floor cleaning robots accounted for 80% of all service robots, with 23.8 million units
Unmanned aerial vehicles accounted for 4 million units
Automated lawnmower units counted 1.6 million units
Automated guided vehicles installed 0.1 million units
Milking robotic units tallied up 0.05 million units

The remaining parts comprised humanoid robots (including assistant/companion robots), telepresence robots, powered human exoskeletons, surgical robots, and autonomous mobile robots. Combined, they were believed to have had fewer than 50,000 units installed.

Humanoid robots, although one of the smaller groups of service robots in the present market have the most potential to become the industrial tool of the future. Companies like Softbank Robotics have produced human-looking robots to be utilized as medical aides and educational aids. Currently, humanoid robots are flourishing in the medical business, notably companion robots.

University of Southern California Professor Maja Matarić has been partnering robots with patients since 2014. Her robots helped youngsters with autism mimic the gestures of socially helpful robots and, in 2015, the robots supported stroke recovery sufferers with upper extremity exercises. The patients were more receptive to the workouts when encouraged and inspired by the robot.

However, firms are increasingly adopting humanoid robots to perform technical responsibilities. A four-year cooperative research effort was done by Joint Robotics Laboratory and Airbus Group to employ humanoid robotic technology in aeroplane production facilities. By putting humanoid robots on aeroplane manufacturing lines, Airbus seeks to relieve human operators of some of the most arduous and risky duties. Human employers might then focus on higher-value activities. The key problem is the tight confines these robots have to operate in and the ability to manoeuvre without clashing with the surrounding things.

The Joint Robotics Laboratory created the new HRP-2 and HRP-4 robot models using a novel robotic movement technique known as multi-contact locomotion. By making use of its full body to make touch with its surroundings, and not just its feet, this sort of robot can climb ladders and access limited locations. The various points of contact on the robot aid to strengthen a robot's stability and give superior force control while completing a job. Lastly, the human shape of these robots allows more adaptability for working in varied contexts.

NASA is deploying its Valkyrie robot for similar duties but on future flights to Mars. Valkyrie is a 6-2 humanoid robot weighing 300 kg. The robot's brain is powered by two Intel Core i7 CPUs, and the head has lidar sensors, cameras, and a Multisense SL camera to constantly scan the surrounding objects and surroundings. The Multisense camera combines laser, 3D stereo, and video to sense the surroundings. Hazard cameras scan forward and behind the torso to identify probable risks.

But the actual worth of Valkyrie lies in its hands. Professor Taskin Padir from Northeastern University and his research team have been in charge of generating human-like flexibility in the robot's hands. "NASA's Valkyrie has three fingers and a thumb on each hand," explains Padir. "Each finger has knuckle-like joints, and each hand has a wrist that can rotate freely. We're focusing on developing motions—combinations of the arm, wrist, finger, and thumb movements that together perform a job, like rotating a wrench in a circle to tighten a bolt, or hauling a cart from one point to another."

The ultimate purpose of robots like Valkyrie is to man the future voyage to Mars. They may be deployed on reconnaissance trips to the planet and employed to build up living compounds, maintaining power and life support systems for future manned expeditions.

So what is lacking for these robots to become more prevalent in all domains of engineering? Two features: flexibility and force control. Currently, robots need specialized programming for each thing they come in touch with. This confines the robots to just one job until they are reprogrammed and re-tasked. Researchers are working on strategies on how to take one robot's programming and apply it to another robot.

The latest machine learning approach from MIT's Computer Science and Artificial Intelligence Laboratory is named C-Learn. The "C" stands for restrictions. C-Learn enables non-coders to teach robots motions and tasks by giving some basic information about the items being controlled and then showing the robot a single demo on how to accomplish the job. "By combining the intuitiveness of learning through demonstration with the accuracy of motion-planning algorithms," says Claudia Pérez-D'Arpino, a PhD student working on the C-Learn project, "robots execute new sorts of tasks that they haven't been able to learn before."

At Columbia University, engineers are exploring new techniques to duplicate human muscle. They have constructed a synthetic muscle that can lift a thousand times its weight, push, pull, bend, and twist. The muscle is a 3D printed combination of silicone rubber matrix with ethanol spread throughout in micro-bubbles and does not need an external compressor or high voltage electrical equipment to work. The muscle is electrically manipulated by employing a thin resistive wire and is low-power (just 8 V) (only 8 V).

Professor Hod Lipson, the team's leader, believes soft material robots show "great promise" for sectors where a gentler touch is necessary. Unlike rigid robots, soft robots can reproduce natural movements, including grabbing and manipulation of items. These additional muscles may be utilized to give medical and other forms of help, execute delicate jobs, or pick up soft items.

"Rather of creating each robot a particular machine specialized for a very specific activity, we need to build multi-use robots—or even such powerful machines that they may be labelled "general purpose" good for practically any work," adds Padir. "Achieving this aim also means designing new designs that integrate hard and soft features —the way human bone offers strength to a grasp, with skin dispersing the pressure so [even] a wine glass doesn't shatter."

Fortunately, there's nothing close to true AI. Cheap computing power has enabled some slick algorithms, but that's all they are. Pornbots are the most sophisticated AI in the wild. The two primary hurdles to true AI are: - Defining intelligence. We understand nearly little about our brains and how we think. When anything goes wrong with our brains our most sophisticated cure is to poke a sharpened stick in there; rearranging things and hoping random chance would result in a good consequence. There are certain laser procedures, but burning a hole or piercing a hole in your head is splitting hairs. We can't remake what we don't comprehend. - Intelligence, as opposed to intelligent calculation, demands the third alternative. That's something a binary system cannot support. At the end of the day, binary algorithms are merely the emulation of a third choice. It's the combining of results from multiple binary calculations. The result is a limited set of alternative outcomes. Granted that finite number might be extremely, really enormous, but it is, nonetheless, finite. I was formerly part of a project where part of the aim was to examine how a really would advertise its arrival as an entity. One of the fundamental parts of every scenario was given a name to itself. A working committee was constituted to theorize how it would arrive at whatever name it picked. As a unique creature, the general opinion was that the AI would want to showcase its unique presence, not fear people to such a degree that its survival would be jeopardized and be something that translated well. There were a few names that fulfilled all the requirements, but the top result was always Jesus Christ! It was hilarious! We couldn't discover any name more likely to terrify people to the point its existence was jeopardized. "I am Jesus Christ and I Am". This was before the term meme was really in the vernacular, but it was a permanent part of the project afterwards. Needless to say, this wasn't included in the final report. It sure was fun though.

And I would add that since our entire economy, social and governmental systems value everyone in terms of their labour - whether it's physical or mental labour - what will happen when robots do even a significant portion of that labour, and eventually all of it? Since the Ship of State (if you will) is massive and hard to turn, people will still be valued by their labour; labour which they have little to no opportunity to perform with all those robots out there. Unable to earn a living, there will be a generation or more of adaptation necessary during which time billions of people will suffer unheard of poverty.

Much of what the Badger had to say is correct. What is missing is all the humans that will, at least for now, design, build, debug, install and service all of those robots. The scary part is the several orders of magnitude growth in AI. Once AI gets to the point of being smarter than humans, humans will no longer need to be part of the system. And that includes all of the engineers, bookkeepers, HR people, Chief Financial Persons and for that matter, the CEO. The impact on us humans will be profound. And then there is the question of the malicious use of AI to create all sorts of nasty things. If you think the Russian hack of the 2016 election was bad, wait for the first evil AI package. I guess that sometime in the next 30 to 75 years human labour will be obsolete!

"...patients responded better when encouraged by a robot". Phenomena completely addressed in Dr Who. More robots are inevitable, but I don't agree with the reasoning behind humanoid robots. I feel the entire problem is being tackled backwards. A robot doesn't need to pull a cart or spin a wrench. In the cart example, the cart itself is the common denominator. It's present regardless of how it is pulled. The cart should drag itself. A robot doesn't need to crank a wrench. Wrenches are levers. Mechanical advantage should come from the robot itself. The present approach to robot design is like placing nonfunctional legs on a robot so it can use a wheelchair. It's not only mimicking human limits, it's destroying an accessory industry and failing to permit substantial advances in the design of other machines. Confined space limitations dissolve. "Wrenching space" for big fasteners is decreased from 2' to 2". The width of traffic lanes on the floor may be decreased by 50% or more and yet give space for big goods. The list is limitless. Anything developed by people has human limits built-in by default. The major money is likely to come from substantial changes. Something to spin a wrench versus someone to turn a wrench is a big incremental gain if you are an accountant. But increasing manufacturing equipment density by 30% in an existing area with more compact machines that can be serviced by robots with minimal safety restrictions is a major advantage if you're the CEO or an engineer. Robots shouldn't be mimicking human limitations. They should be boosting expectations.

www.ingramcontent.com/pod-product-compliance
Lightning Source LLC
LaVergne TN
LVHW022126060326
832903LV00063B/4794